Memoirs

A story of life, sex, and finding faith in numbers.

To the one that I never followed through in lust, but I have always loved our friendship. Todd. Life would not have been near as fun. Thank you for the ever-lasting support, late nights, drinks, endless laughs, love, advice, and the occasional teenage crush. Here's to decades of thanking God for the "friend zone."

Introduction.

I set down to write this book about two years before I did so. One night, two years later. after hearing Bob Segar's Hollywood Nights." A song that will forever take me back to so many nights, happy nights, nights I was full. I set in my car, four kids, three dogs, journey to God, and a husband later, I realized my idea of full was now, much more filling. At that moment, I knew I finally had the mindset to sit down and tell this story. This story isn't every chapter, but it's the ones that stuck. The ones that made me grow in so many ways. On the surface, I grew up in perfect, small town USA. I was in sports, choir, went to homecoming, went to the parties, had friends and a decent homelife. On the backside of this surface, I was a bi racial girl, raised by two women, in a time where it was not exactly welcoming.

I found peace on my own as a child that had dealt with sexual abuse (as an adult physical abuse) I found peace with realizing racism is not my fault, and freedom comes when you learn to say, "fuck off," and live for yourself.

But this story? Doesn't touch most of that, it's my love story, my way

Part 1

"All The Queens Men Couldn't Put Her Back Together Again"

To me love isn't what drives us early on, it is the giddy feeling, the lust, the excitement, the hot passion that leaves after three months, then we are onto the next. That's what led me to believe, bleed, hate, heal, play, and finally find the love that lasted past any number or passing emotion.

One.

Something to always be said about the first person who brought you puppy love, that first feeling of butterflies.

I met Tai when I was in middle school, before braces, before sex. He was innocent, he was sweet natured, and he gave me all the butterflies a tween aged girl could want. I learned later in life, that my devouring nature as a woman led Tai to avoid women like me all together. We had a kiss, we held hands, and as most middle school loves go, that was all.

Ten years after that first, innocent, kiss; his eyes became my favorite shade of blue. Tai liked to drink and play air guitar to songs, dance with me, laugh with me, tease me. We spent many nights, listening to rock, snorting lines of cocaine in the town bar bathroom, drinking, and just being lost. I was never sure of his intentions, but he knew mine. Something about him made me question just why I never gave in and acted right. Dozens of kisses and touches later, I took him into me, anywhere he would have me, beds, floors, bathrooms.

One night, outside, on a reconstructed porch, he shoved me against the door of the house, I breathed him in and lost my train of thought. His eyes did not gleam that favorite color, but glared heat into my returning gaze. I did not care where, I just wanted him, and the urge and feeling never stifled. I lusted after him in ways that didn't have to be spoken.

Every inch of him, physically and mentally, down to his laugh and smile to the parts that give me pleasure. I craved him. Some months into it, I felt him pull away, the "why" was never asked, nor answered. I saw him so many days after we parted and that feeling, that urge, that want, still set at the edge of my throat, body, and soul. So much in fact, even in my fucked-up head, it was best to stay back and let him be. I ended up seeing someone else for quite some months after, just to numb what I wanted from Tai. At the time and even now I could not tell you what I ever wanted.

Took me years, to understand sometimes that lust masks as love.

Because it comes into your life just like love, to teach you, to move you, and then it's gone. Leaving you emptier than love ever could, because the reality was never there to begin with. All that was left was this mask covered lust, playing those endless nights, on repeat in your head, as the what if's blared the soundtrack.

Two.

Once I discovered that cocaine and nicotine brought me up and out? I didn't look back, I staggered, blurry eyed, forward and anyone who didn't move with me? I ran over, breaking hearts, souls, and intentions along the way. Not many people survived this, I know I didn't.

My freshman year I met Van. Van was two years older than I, he was the athlete, the drug dealer, the friend, the boyfriend, the clown, the partner in crime, to almost everyone the years he was front and center in my life. He was all of those to me, except boyfriend. He was my midnight call for coke and sex, he was my spring break fueled by LSD, coke, and a lot of long nights. He had an equally popular girlfriend and I had a very distracted, sweet freshman boyfriend who trusted me, (his mistake).

Van made me forget all responsibility, loyalty, and emotion. Well, I had emotion, but it was like a horrible, story problem, with all these factors I didn't see at first, nor did I want to.

Factors: Emotions, sex, drugs.

Horrible story problem: Emotions deeper than lust-got cancelled out or masked by the drugs-the drugs were heightened by the sex-bringing me back to what I though was love. Turns out it was just sex and sex was the basis of our relationship, oh and drugs, did I mention that?

Van was irritating, unattainable, and gorgeous all at once. For a miniscule, school girl moment, I thought maybe, we could have been more.

The night that moment and any lingering emotion passed, was a night, he told me to stick out my tongue and put a hit of acid on it. It was two years into our on and off cycle of sex, drugs, lies, repeat. I remember sitting on his lap, I remember him leaving saying he would be right back. The next thing I remember is seeing black.

The black came in and out as the blows to my head came, one...two..three. I remember fighting back and trying to run, the acid trip no longer front in my mind, I turned to see another girl beside me unconscious, as I rolled over trying to shake her awake, another force, this time pulling my hair, whipping my head back. I tasted blood and my face went numb. A deep voice, whispered in my ear as I struggled to free myself.

"Not tonight, why don't you just stay down like a good girl," the whisper in my ear came from behind my body, that now felt a 1,000 pounds heavier.

A guy I barely knew but whose face I had seen before sneered up at me from over the girl's body. The stranger behind breathed in my ear, I thought I shuttered but I couldn't tell, " why don't you watch right now, " As I tried to scream out his hands tightened on my hair and yanked my head ack up. As my mind further registered what was about to happen I begin to vomit..

and black.

Police, lights, questions, charges, death.

I remember seeing Van run to me from the long drive that led to the house steps I was sitting on.

I remember him trying to jump in the back of the ambulance, yelling "who did this?!" over and over, the police, coming over to take him away, as he's screaming, "not her, where is he?!" repeatedly until it echoed in my mind, even when I finally slept.

I blocked out the part of calling my mother who was three states away at the time, a mother who never knew I was ever into drugs or sex.
Her heart broke over the phone during that 45 minute conversation and again when she made it home.

One week of silence, one suicide later, I came back to school, I came back to life, or so I thought.
The word rape, center in my head.

The word victim making me cringe every time it left someone's lips.

I realized, though I was going through the motions, I was even more of a shell of who I was before. The left side of my face had slight muscle and nerve damage and still to this day, I have a crooked smile. I walked the halls with bruising on my jawline and eye for about two to three weeks after. My hair in two braids to hide the bald spots where my hair was ripped out.

For every day of silence, there was a voicemail or a note, from Van. My Mother, to this day says he was the devil and the angel that night, though with more remorse than anyone.

One of the guys, jock friends of Van's, hung himself the day after the charges were pressed, the other?

Thanks to Van was charged, put in jail, and lost all scholarships and freedom for time last I heard he and his family moved out of state.

I thank God, now, that my story was cut, dry, and justice was served. I feel it led me to a road of healing (not right away) that most victims of this very thing do not often receive. I am a black hole of things I kept to myself or blocked out. Until I met my husband, I never knew how severe that hole was. Van wasn't my hero, but after that, he was the friend who didn't sell me drugs, didn't see me for sex. He saw me for movie dates, and let me talk to him on the phone, and two years and more he still is the one that we can pick up like we have never left off.

In those days, I realized I was not the only one who harbored different feelings, but after that night, that notion would never be. My emotions for Van ran deeper until, I found I could never love him more than the silent heartbreak surrounding my soul. A heartbreak that set in every time I saw him, a heartbreak I never told him about. Because my fear was the truth, the heartbreak was not even. He lost touch with a girl he never saw more than a good friend, that he had let down, and that kept him from me on every intimate level. I never had the nerve to speak of love to him, and after the dark, the black, that soaked my memories, we have spoken of that night, only once.

"I never would have-," "I know,"

"You have to know I would never let-, "

"I know,"

"God damn it Sydney, I'm so fucking sorry,"

"Van?" "I know."

That was it, book closed. Now, we have seen each other through our children being born, good relationships, bad relationships, college and careers. That night, was blurry and lost for me in parts, due to the physical pain, blows to my head, and emotional lack of healing. Nevertheless, I have dealt with that night and threw it away.

The numbers ahead were caught in that fire. You see for a long time after that I never tied sex with emotion, ever. I don't care who I was to you, you were literally just a number to me. Rather it be in the days you kept me around, or the places I screwed you (physically or mentally), or the number of times we had sex. Just a number. My memories came in flashbacks and numbers, from numbers of orgasms, to convos, to touches, to names, to age, all numbers.

As for the one that moved me, the number that left me empty and full at the same time; Van saw my numbers and raised me his own. At the end of the innocence lost story, we never forfeited our friendship. Through the wanting, the drugs, the sex, the roller-coaster of pure bullshit that was high school we had seen each other through everything, like I said. In our own twisted way, a way no one will quite ever understand, we are forever connected. Not all love stories end in some intimate, romantic gesture. There was a sunset, but there was no prince, not this time, no.

There was just Van and memories that flooded the entire sky.

Three. Four. Five. Six.

The rebounds, the in between' s, the fun ones, the embarrassing ones, the sad ones. The ones who get us over the emotional hump of whatever we are trying to fight internally. For a long time that was my life, my story, my seven days a week, passing time, life. A time that monogamy was a ridiculous notion. A time where I felt souls connect, not in twos, but in whatever I found reasonable. Long nights of tequila and endless hours of play and self- hatred.

There was a substitute teacher, when I was 18 and he was 23. We spent the time having sex and playing games and enjoying each other. We were a lot alike, we joked, and jabbed at each other, we liked sports and rap music. The sex was even fun as he was literally 14 inches taller than me. Rough and fun, and wanted, our days went fast.

We just played, and that was the best way to describe our time. He called me up one day talking about a waitress he met and I said with true happiness in my voice, "enjoy," and to this day we are distant friends.

There was a younger brother and an older brother, Ike and Zane. The younger Ike satisfied my sexual appetite, while the older Zane, satisfied my mind. I'd spend hours with the Ike tangled up, down, all around, letting him have me and devour me only to watch him leave and chase after other girls. While I spent the rest of the night with Zane, talking, driving around, listening to the rain and nighttime country sounds.

One summer night, Zane came in slamming doors yelling at his younger brother to grow up and treat me right. Ike left immediately, shaking his head, explaining to Ike that is not what he and I were about. The quiet in the room after Ike left brought an ache in my stomach I had not felt in a while.

I knew then Zane was not interested in our convos alone. I remember grazing his face with my fingers, and him grabbing me up to kiss me. After the kiss, I knew the ache was not for me. It was pity for him and him alone. I left and went driving alone that night and never spoke of them or to them from that night on.

There was JJ.

JJ was a powerful man at a powerful company many miles away. I met him at a quiet bar in Indy on one of his many trips back to his hometown. We bonded over a favorite TV show and stories of past lovers.

Seemed easy enough, and simple enough. I should have taken it as a universal warning that I could never relax around him. He made me uneasy, I thought it was the sexual tension between us, the wanting and waiting until we could have each other. He would have me tie him up and leave him for hours and come back and make him kiss me and touch me and he wanted me to slap him. He wanted me to control him, in his words he spent all day running the show and controlling all around him, he wanted the intimate time to be different. When I would untie him he would take my head in his hands and kiss me passionately.

Even then, I could not relax, finally after weeks of buildup, and bondage, we planned a night out. I was expecting a simple dinner and back to my place routine, but he brought me to a party with several friends from his hometown. Several had girlfriends, some did not, and that's when I saw him. Cale.

Seven??

Cale, nodded when we were introduced, was loud and outgoing with the men and quiet and polite with the ladies, never overlooking, overstepping or anything less.

He was clean cut, innocence oozing out of every word loud or soft he spoke.

I wanted to ruin him.

I wanted to run my hands through his hair and shove my tongue down his throat every time he just had to be polite and courteous to me.

When JJ was preoccupied on his phone, I purposefully struck up a conversation with Cale. He let me in a little, explaining how he knew JJ (childhood friends and college roommates) and flipped the convo to how I knew him, as I was about to reply, JJ returned and the night took a shift back just to convo and drinks. I couldn't take my eyes away from him when he spoke. He wasn't well put together like the other guys.

He was jeans and t shirt...and well.... he just screamed.... geek.

His complete being made me smile in a way I had not in so long. JJ and I fizzled out not even a month later (my nerves never let it go, so friend zone he went). Though we still had a good time grabbing drinks and just enjoying some laughs and convo, the uneasy feeling was no longer if we just remained friends.

Parties and gatherings and food went on for months and holidays, I got closer to JJ's circle and enjoyed the company. Each gathering drawing me closer to Cale, learning about his family, (he had three brothers and was the middle son), learning he came from a very prominent family in the same small town setting I grew up in.

At the time I did not believe in God, and he was raised catholic and that made for some interesting conversations. He said one day that I would understand and there wouldn't be all these questions. I would laugh and roll my eyes.

It would take me 17 years to know just how right he was. You see my darkness was not always bold and forthcoming, but it was always at my surface. 17 years and those conversations were single handedly the reason I let it all go and faced peace head on.

I remember it being a Saturday, another party. The sky was deep and bright even into the night. Brightened by the moon of the night and the stars. Cale was leaving and I decided to call it a night at the same time.

I should tell you, flirty? Me? Yes. But my mind never worked overtime in the being "straight forward," category until years later. I tended to be very immature and childlike with dating. A horrible mind set when playing with people's emotions.

As he walked me to me car and stood beside me as I sat down and turned my key, I remember feeling safe, warm. For the first time, I did not see him as a conquest, I saw him. His eyes were a shade of green and blue and deeper than any conversation I had probably ever held.

Before my mind had an ounce of time to think, my mouth blurted out, "I think I like you," to which he responded, "I like you too Syd."

"So now what?" I had a hard time keeping eye contact with him, and that never changed. But when I looked up at his face, so serious and forward, I feared the answer was not what I wanted to hear.

Instead a tiny smiled appeared at the edge of his lips,

"Well I haven't got that far, but it probably needs to start with telling my childhood best friend, I am falling for the girl he brought to the party."

"Yes." Slightly disappointed didn't hide in my tone. "Can I see you tomorrow?" Damn the mouth.

"I can try, and I want to, but I have to talk to Jay. Syd, I have to."

I never asked about the convo, for Cale's sake I cared enough to understand friendship was first.

A friendship of his and JJ's caliber, would trump any female. I was fine with that. I could respect that. But for reasons beyond what my damaged soul could not see at the time, I could not let him go. There was no number. There was not a bone in my body that wanted to run from him.

No, I never ask about the conversation between them.

Not even a day later, my phone lit up. I answered.

"So your favorite ice cream is strawberry?"

I smiled, "Sure is,"

"I can see you at six with ice cream?"

"Absolutely. "

I remember hanging up and smiling pretty much for the remainder of the day. Young and dumb does not hold a candle to young and in lust and maybe, love?

"Only Happy People Understand Love."

Days went on, nights went to fast, we led a path filled with heavy kisses and deep conversations. Conversations about religion and the constellations, conversations about sex and friendships, parents, pets, everything. He was a man of faith who was saving himself for marriage.

I had many questions, and arguments; all starting out something along the lines of, "what if the sex is bad and you're stuck?" I know now my mind was to small, spiritually to grasp the concept. I kept my mouth shut and for the first time in a long time, I forgot the bad, I forgot about the past, I forgot about Van, and the numbers that followed. I saw him and I saw perfect. Even in disagreement, I managed to stay in harmony with Cale. He would spend his weekdays working 1-2 hours away, and at night Id find a way to sneak into his arms.

Before either of us knew it, we found ourselves in love. I remember one particular night, a power outing was spent listening to him play guitar as I laid at his feet brought a burning inside that I had never felt.

Days and nights spent under a manipulating summer sky. Days turned into weeks; weeks turned into months.

The nights, the dinners, the surprises, the laughter, the wanting, kept me at that time and kept me for a while, I was mature enough not to have sex. I wanted him, but I loved him and respected him more than my own beliefs. He was unlike anyone I had ever met, that much was screaming obvious. I was unlike anyone he had ever met only because, unlike the other females, I stuck around after the no sex until marriage talk.

Yes, I stuck around and my eyes didn't wander, he didn't wander, but all this rise to relationship maturity for me, was a like a stage show, real and raw while speaking, but when the curtains closed the character was left on stage as I walked away. I wanted to love him correctly, but my soul, my heart, my mind, well we were never ready. Looking back, I think he was sent to me to heal my heart and open my mind.

One day, in late July, after dinner, we were laying by the water, a quiet summer day, 80 but not scorching, slight breeze, my head tipped back taking in the sun, it was perfect. I felt him go quiet, the silence was so blatant it almost screamed out to me. I knew something was off. But I kept my head tilted taking in the sun, pretending to keep the normalcy.

"What are your thoughts on marriage?" He knew this one, this was a test, tread lightly, is all I could think.

"I'm not sure, monogamy seems to be such a fluid concept for so many people, even some in relationships, why is marriage always the finish line?"

I could see the irritation sitting at the edge of his face..creeping in.

"Commitment is the finish line, levels of intimacy, not physical, but mental, that's the finish line." "A partner, a spouse, you commit to for life and build with." "THAT'S the finish line." He emphasized the words with such force, I snapped my head up.

"Does this conversation have a point beyond starting an argument?" I said at that point, equally irritated, so much for treading lightly.

"Why does it have to be an argument with you?" "I am genuinely asking."

"You've asked before, and it's not an argument but I can hear the frustration in your tone, I can feel it in the fucking air, hell I'm sure the fish in the damn pond can feel your mood." "Were you expecting a different answer?"

"Syd its been over six months of course I expect a different answer." "I'm not asking you to miraculously change your entire belief system, I just thought that maybe this certain view," he paused.

"Would change because of us?" I finished for him.

"Well, yeah, I mean I love you." "I'm in love with you." He said quietly, his blue eyes dark.

I let the silence sit for a minute..felt like an hour. I needed to speak, I needed to woman up and reassure this man, I was not leaving, I was just as in love. I wanted to tell him. But my irritation took over before my heart did.

"You know, I love you." "I want you, only you." "So what if we don't rush down the God damn aisle."

"Will you stop loving me?" I got up and started to walk back towards the trail to go back to the house.

"I got a job offer in Tennessee."

I stopped dead in my tracks, bricks flew through my chest. What. The. Fuck. Was all that ran through my mind.

"Is that what this is all about?" I walked back towards him.

"Yes." "And I knew you'd get all huffy and upset."

"I am NOT huffy." "I'm pissed off, you thought your little test question would be a nice way to tell me you may be fucking leaving the state." "I knew that question was a trap."

"I am not trying to trap you with a conversation about the future or potential future we could have, ever." 'If you that's how you see it then we have a bigger problem than a job two states away."

I took a deep breath. "Ok, start over, this job?"

"It's 80,000 a year, doing what I do here, but I lead my own crew, and many other benefits." "They don't want me to start until March of the new year."
"It could be a great opportunity...for both of us." "I want you to come with me."

"You want to live with me before marriage?" I said with a very mocking tone.

"Well. What do you think about our one year being a different kind of date?" his smile was halfcocked.

Like he knew the gamble he was taking and was not one ounce scared of the loss if it fell apart. This was a rare cockiness I saw in him, and it always made me want him more, it made me shut up instantly. I knew I had lost this convo. My jaw had to have fallen, because he stepped right on front of me and his fingers pushed my chin up.

"I've never wanted anyone more than I want you, you challenge me, you love me, you want me, just me, for myself."

"Are you proposing?"

"Let's call it a lifetime promise question? "Proposal, sounds way to much like a legal proposition." He said winking.

A million thoughts and questions, was it to soon? Was it just a hurried answer to having sex with a woman he loved? What if I failed him? What if he failed? What if the sex wasn't anything? I loved him. I fell fast and hard in love with this man for so many other reasons and so much more than sex. But what if...

All these thoughts and all I could say...

"I can accept a lifetime promise."

The biggest smile spread across his face and he scooped me up in his arms and twirled me around.

I don't remember the months that followed, it was a simple, happy, bubble. A bubble that floated along, until one fucking night. One fucking, crazy, reckless, night. The bubble popped, my world exploded yet again.

"So I'll come by and see you again, I'll be just a very good friend, I will not look upon your face, I will not touch upon your grace, your ecclesiastic skin."
  -M.Ethridge

Three weeks before our "promise," date and seven weeks before our move, life was busy. Our friends had decided to throw us a joint party to celebrate the upcoming events. They rented out a bar/restaurant in the heart of city. We took limo rides and got all dressed up, laughs, smiles, convos surrounding us all, it was a beautiful evening.

"Syd, I would like you to meet my cousin Damien." Cale's arm wrapped around my waist, he extended the other arm out to the gentleman in front of me.

Damien was tall, handsome, and had eyes that spoke of devious thoughts even if his mouth never did. I wasn't impressed by this, I was cautious. Something irritated me about him from the very way he shook my hand.

"Hello, I said with a smile, dropping his hand almost immediately.

"Well little cousin, why don't we take a shot all of this good news."

"I think I've had enough," Cale responded with a smile.

"One shot with the cousin you never see?" "Maybe even one for the future Mrs?"

I rolled my eyes, "Sure one shot, so you'll maybe leave it alone."

"Whoa, well done cousin, got yourself a spicy Latina." He said jokingly, as he winked in my direction. He disgusted me.

Cale laughed, "Ok, one shot."

Four shots later, I stopped counting and the rude cousin left. I had never seen Cale so loose and well, drunk.

I needed water and a bathroom; I remember pep talking myself into not throwing up. My dress was satin and deep red with a slit, I had lost my shoes somewhere. I stumbled into the bathroom door, as Cale was coming out.

"Oh, goodness, sorry future wife." He smiled staggering.

I smiled back and threw my hands around his neck and planted a loud kiss on his lips. We both slid back into small bathroom.

I separated myself from him, to look at him.

"Let me..leave..so." His words all over the place. Whew, he was trashed.

"Give me another kiss and I'll let you go."

He leaned in and I grabbed his face, I could smell his cologne mixed with whiskey.

I wanted him. God, I wanted him bad, the alcohol brought every physical want straight to my surface.

As I kissed him his hands wondered down to my hips and kept lowering. I felt how hard he was against my body and stopped his hands.

"I'll let you go-

His mouth was on mine feverishly, he spun me around, picked me up and sat me onto the sink.

He found my dresses slit with his hand and ran his hand up my thigh. He began pleasuring me with his hands and then his mouth.

I could have stopped him, I should have stopped him, his virtue was of utmost importance, his family was right outside, our wedding was so close, our promise, his promise, our future....alcohol wasn't all to blame, I should have stopped him.

Instead I guided his hands, pushed myself against his tongue as he went down on me, only stopping to take his pants off and pleasure him softly with my mouth before taking him inside of me. Letting him have me for as long as the whiskey was letting him. Letting him cum inside me at the very same moment I let go.

We didn't say anything as we came out, him staggering out first. I, suddenly aware my dress was a mess, drunkenly fixed my hair and walked out.

Goodbyes, good lucks, and two hours, and one quiet taxi ride later, we came to my house. He never stayed, he always went home, for obvious reasons. I looked at him and he smirked eyes half open.

I opened the taxi door and he wasn't two steps behind with the sack that held the bottle of whiskey and two engraved glasses gifted to us from the bar.

"Are you staying?"

He kissed my cheek, missing my mouth, nodded. We barely made it in the door before he was reaching for my hips, pulling me into him again.

But this time I didn't guide him anywhere, clothes were taken off as he took me from behind against the front door, and again on the couch. Over and over, exploring more and more.

I'd like to tell you that the next morning, there was conversation, an embrace over coffee, an understanding and a guilt free air. I would like to tell you, I was a big enough person to understand that I handled the next morning with graciousness and understanding. But that would make both statements a lie, a huge, monumental, lie.

Looking back, I only remember bits and pieces, I shut out a lot over the years, rather it was from guilt or anger, the point was it was no longer taking space in my head. Now, it is just a feeling of I have moved on, but it felt like lifetimes before I reached that destination over this night.

There was slight yelling, I remember telling him there was obviously no God in how he acted and maybe he should ask for forgiveness (of course I was being a smartass).

"How dare you, blame me for this," I was now all but snarling words as they just kept flying from my mouth.

"I never said I blamed you, I'm just as much to blame, but everything, every day, every prayer I worked for, I prayed for," He was scattered and he was angry.

"Oh, so life is over now?" "Because you had SEX WITH YOUR FIANCE?" I was angrily, picking up the living room now to distract myself from making eye contact. I remember being so angry, and then my stomach sinking.

"For fucks sake Syd, can you just slow down, calm down!" He grabbed both of my arms and made me look him in the eye.

"I know you don't understand and it's my fault for not making you-"

"Making me?" "I'm not an idiot Cale,"

"That's not what I mean, give me damn minute, I'm just saying this is my entire belief system and now its wrecked."

"This was my life, my morals."

"So you regret it?" I said now in a low tone.

"Of course, I do," he barely whispered back. "How can you not see how this makes my world different?"

"All I see is a man who finally got sex and now regrets it." I stepped back; I could feel my skin heating up.

"You regret me."

"Syd-" I cut him off.

"Get the fuck out of my house." "Call your perfect parents and tell them that their perfect son fucked up, and they need to cancel everything."

"GET THE FUCK OUT NOW."

"Fine." He whispered. No fight, no more yelling, he just said "fine," and walked out my door.

I collapsed as soon as he left, hitting the floor, sobbing. I was so angry, irate. Looking back, gosh, what a child. What a small minded, hopeless, child.

Everything went black, but this time, there was no blow to the head, there was no physical trauma.

Only that heartbreak, only this ache. Phone calls from parents, friends, explain and lying that it didn't work out because we just were too different, trying to make sense of it while trying to defend my choice.

I was stupid.

Selfish.

Everything. Went. Black.

One Month.
Three Months.
Six Months.

"..If you're losing your soul and know it, then you've still got a soul left to lose" -Charles Bukowski

I remember going through the motions, I remember cutting my hair, changing my clothing style, my perfume scent, my lotion, everything I could do just to strip away... him, this heartache. It would be three months before I got the nerve to call him, sadly, I don't remember the convo. I know it ended.

I know he married a nice woman later in life. I know she was everything his mother wanted. I know she is the exact opposite of me from the skin tone to the blonde hair.

To this day, he avoids me when I see him. Its like we never were. It used to sting, until I came to the realization, you can't always play with fire and come out unscathed. That entire time I cried, ached, and hated him, I never considered he was the one who got burnt, not me. I never took in consideration he had two heartbreaks on that dreaded day, one morally he would never be able to forgive himself for, one physically losing a woman he thought he knew and loved.

Mentally I was light years behind that kind of maturity at that moment. I stripped him away from my soul, in the process, I came to a very difficult conclusion....I needed to find mine.

Fading..

"She was beautiful, passionate, and as crazy as I was, she could party like a man, and love like a woman"

-"Blow"

And the numbers continued.. I was alone, single, and finally aware, I could not keep coming home and listening to the same sad songs and watching the same sad movies. I called up some friends and decided to venture out for an evening.

How cliché, right? It was.

Cliché brought me to a very big night club, cliché brought me to run into a girl by accident, causing her drink to spill down my black mini dress.

"Oh shit, I am so sorry." Her long waist length dark hair, twirling around as she whipped her head up to look at me.

"No, let me buy you a drink this is all my fault," I began to ramble on about how I should not be out, and I stopped.

Her head was cocked slightly, and her skin tone was olive, dark eyes looking me up and down with a smirk. She stood barely 5'3 and prob not 100 pounds. So tiny next to my 5'6, athletic build.

"Tell you what, I'll shut up, and I'll buy you a replacement drink and we can go our separate ways." I smiled.

"I TELL YOU WHAT," she replied with a huge grin, "come with me, and my guy will buy us both drinks and you and your friends can come sit and you finish telling me why you shouldn't have come out."

I smiled, something about her, I didn't want to say no. "My name is Nadia, we are over here at the VIP stage."

"Syd," I replied with a half-smile.

I grabbed my two girlfriends and away we went, as I stepped up into the VIP area, I familiar voice called out.

"Well, well, I never thought I'd see you again."

My eyes quickly found him, Damien, and his arm rested gently around Nadia's shoulders.

I wanted to puke, I wanted to turn and run, and I went to grab my girlfriends arm and do just that.

"Oh great, you've met!" Nadia exclaimed with utter joy.

He smiled, that smile, I hated. He was still handsome, gorgeous in fact, chiseled features and muscles that outlined under his shirt.

"You could say that," he smirked, and that was it.

Nadia grabbed my arm and pulled me to the couch next to her.

"So spill." She smiled, hand on my knee.

Without detail I just explained it was my first night out since a breakup and that led to everything from where I was from, where she was from, how she met Damien, to dancing, and more drinks, and more dancing, and more drinks.

Before I knew it, it was three in the morning and we were following them to their apartment in the city for the after party. I felt free, distracted, and it was all because if this woman. This tiny, outspoken, wild, woman.

My two girlfriends passed out on the couch about an hour later, as I staggered to the bathroom, I walked In Damien doing a line of coke.

He looks up, smiles, and hands me the straw. As he does so Nadia opens the door behind us, the bathroom attached to the main bedroom, "Oh goody, I wondered if you'd be joining us."

She quickly snags the straw and runs playfully back towards the bedroom. Damien grabs my hand and leads me to their bedroom. Lights dim, music still blaring from the living room, Nadia grabs my face and kisses me. Stunned, I look to Damien.

"No worries," he says smoothly, "she's wanted you all night."

"Oh?" is all I could manage. I wasn't scared, I was curious, I kissed her back.

She took her dress off and laid back on the bed. Damien took his clothes off, cut two lines of coke and laid them out just below her belly button. He fed her a line from his hand and laid down beside her.

"Care to join us?" He said lifting the straw towards me. I was stunned but the alcohol buzz kept my poker face.

I undressed, slowly as they both watched, and grabbed the straw.

Line after line, Damien would watch her and I touch, lick, and kiss each other all over. Until he grabbed me from behind, I felt his strength in his hands grabbing my waist, for a moment, I forgot about Nadia, turned to face him, and let him go deeper, he was insanely gorgeous, and all the hate surfaced into a sexual drug fueled night. We had what felt like hour after hour of sexual encounters.

Me, Nadia, Damien, repeat.

Coming down, I went to crash as my girlfriends woke up to call a cab, I remember telling them, I was going to sleep a bit more at home as we walked out the door.

Im pretty sure sleep didn't find me for three more days, because by 3pm the next day, I was back at Nadia and Damiens place.

All I could see, breathe, and want was Nadia. We stayed up snorting coke and having sex with each other anywhere we could. We would laugh and tell each other stories, when the coke would be gone, Damien would provide more. I masked any remaining ache with Nadia and my ex fiancés cousin. Rock bottom wasn't where I was, I was in a hell I never saw coming nor wanted to leave.

Damien was the alchemist mixing all of my emotions and never letting me bubble over in one thought or the other, but he knew I was always on the verge. I found my fascination with him was the same way. His very taste rolled off my tongue, even still I never did care for his conversation or his presence much.

One month into our hellacious bliss, I was alone with Damien and it led to him giving me oral sex on the living room floor as Nadia walked in the door, she hurled her body at Damien and started screaming and clawing at him, saying "this is mine," over and over to the point of being hysterical, nose bleeding from what I can only assume was the coke she had been doing elsewhere, drawing scratches on Damien's chest with every slap.

The fight led to him and her having sex in front of me. The crazy part was I saw nothing wrong in her or him, the sheer toxicity of this relationship should have sent me running, not to mention the fact if Cale ever knew. His name hadn't entered my head in so long, I shuddered when it came across my mind.

The next night, Damien didn't come home, Nadia packed up her things and begged me to come back to New York with her, not coked out, but high on hurt and emotion, she told me she loved me and we could be together alone there.

"I cant do that Nadia, I —" She put her hand up, she knew I couldn't love her like she wanted, frankly, I don't think she wanted me either, I was just another person to go down the rabbit hole with. I walked her to the cab, kissed her head and said good bye.

I saw my reflection in the cab window and gulped. I was at least 15 pounds lighter and my muscle tone seemed almost gone.

I went back upstairs, laid my key on the table Nadia had given me, dumped out the cocaine left in my purse and I left. Within three days, I heard from Nadia and then I never heard from her again. Rumor has it she had a child and is living in Florida.

As for Damien? Married with children and we have never spoken again.

Going home that day was this giant sigh of relief and also like hitting a wall. I had to face myself sober, alone, and now with this enormous guilt.

Part Two Rebirth.

"Power is Being Told You Are Not Loved and Not Being Destroyed By It"
- Madonna

Back then I couldn't see past the end of my nose. I told you I could, I told you I could see lifetimes and futures. I would tell some my home life was simply to much and that's why, or that I just didn't care. Your feelings weren't mine so therefore I did not feel the need to not hurt you or dispose of you.

I would tell lies for money, lies for comfort, lies for love, just so I would seem like this carefree, together soul. When in fact I just lost and drowning and it was complete bullshit.

The truth was, I hurt first so I would not be the one getting hurt. The sheer self sabotage of it all, was an immature play. Trauma danced on-the edges, sure, but the choices, the moves, were always mine. I never felt attachment to anything beyond a certain amount of time. Commitment didn't scare me, getting hurt, did, losing did.

Ok, maybe commitment did scare me, maybe. Maybe the sheer thought of sharing my soul, having to stop and consider another being was despicable to me.

It disgusted me when friends would comment about how they dress up for their man, or "their partner wouldn't like it they were out at the club dancing all the time with strangers."

Who the fuck were these people? Who were these so called great people that made you change everything about yourself. I found this behavior weak and belittling.

Women "bowing" to men. To anyone.

Only because my immature brain couldn't wrap around the simplicity of these statements. These friends weren't bowing, they were having fun with their partner and respecting their partner.

I used to consider myself a guys girls, partying, playing, not caught up in "dumb girl stuff," as I called it. Always putting down these type of girls.
Even though I was out here playing with fire at every angle.

These next numbers were not lovers,not conquests, but hard truths, I had to learn. Years of being tied up at my own hands..these truths were the beginning of my undoing... my rebirth.

1. Loyalty

At the base of every single wrong, is a slap at loyalty. Rather it's those donuts on your diet, or secretly emotionally attaching yourself to a person, who is not your partner. It's an attack on loyalty.

People shy away from loyalty often because it simply means they have to be true to themselves to be true to someone else. Inevitably we are running from ourselves when we give empty promises, and a love we will speak out loud but never really live up to.

Only people who truly, healthily love themselves succeed in loyal, committed, anything.

I ran from my own reflection for years. Loneliness was the ultimate drug and I mixed it with bad lovers, hurting the good lovers, bullshit lies and chaos.

My loyalty got lost in translation. I was either loyal to the wrong people or to whoever I wanted near me at the time for my own selfish reasons.

The result?

Karma in the form have never having a faithful lover. Never having a true friend. Never having full faith in myself or anything.

Karma aka God trying to show me over and over again my true worth and me ignoring it like a fool and moving onto the next heartbreak or wrong doing. You can't put ugly and non truths out in the world and expect loyalty back.

You can weed out the bad. The bad friends who suck your soul empty or just ride with you while life is good. Weed out the lovers who do the same. Give your word, your truth, your loyalty to a relationship (friends and lover alike) that makes you better.

Makes you better by giving you peace and comfort. Someone who respects you and your goals, dreams, sobriety , sexuality. Someone who says the words "I'm here for you," and means it.

Give your loyalty to your job, your pet, yourself. Don't bend or compromise this.

Your word is your loyalty and your words followed by action is what represents your character and your character should never be questioned.

2. Forgiveness.

You should forgive. Period.

Forgive him, her, them, they, yourself.

Forgiveness in any form is the first step of moving forward. I think so many people are quit to not forgive because they have the misconception that to forgive is to make the wrong done to them seem, excusable. Or the bad decisions okay.

No. Forgiveness is the art of moving forward, taking a lesson with you, so you are never to make that mistake again.

Forgiving someone who has done you wrong is a great and triumphant task, because you're no longer letting that person take up space in your heart, mind, soul.

Forgiveness is never saying "okay," to a situation that has hurt you.

It took me a monumental amount of time to forgive myself for the hurt I had caused people, the lies I lived. Mentally I felt 1,000 years old, trying to shake the feeling I was a disappointment to anything and everything I touched. I had been in such unhealthy relationships that I felt I couldn't even share my true feelings. I was told I was selfish or indulgent for wanting a " hug or physical touch." I wasn't allowed to speak intelligently without being mocked for it. Couldn't dare be in a bad mood when the world had bled me dry. My mind was strong even still, but it was now warped.

Forgiving those lovers was required to move forward.

Forgiving myself for hurting others, was the only way the black hole in my chest didn't deepen and the warped fog mindset, was lifted.

3. You Cannot Have Growth and Keep Your Bullshit

Frankly, this one was harder for me than I thought. This hard truth stemmed from a night, after I got my shit together, I met up with old friends , we all had our careers, our dogs, spouses, dogs, kids, whatever else adults can bring to a table to converse about.

I was asked about how the writing process was going and twang experiment I was putting on paper. Most of these convos were therapeutic for me. It no longer hurt to talk about painful memories and lessons, so it was all, " book publishing is fun," "adulting is the best," etc, etc.

Lots of laughs, catching up, then I noticed when one old friend would bring up moronic bs in the convo that I did, or we did, (but mostly pointed out mine), I stopped laughing.

Truth is I had grown enough not to laugh off these things, young and dumb was no joke for some of us, I am and have been fully aware of my bad moments.

Said friend always brings up same stories and laughs them off. I don't know if this is her way of dealing with her own bullshit, but I no longer lived in that hamster wheel.

So I smiled, my love for her still lingers because she was a part of my life for so long, but I no longer sought out her approval. I no longer needed that connection from her I always felt I needed as a teen/young adult. I was no longer the angry teenager, or the quiet 20 something to her loud and hurt demeanor.

She too, had demons, skeletons, instead of facing any of them, she blamed the small town and let the trauma dictate her life. She had zero growth. She had a degree, she had a career, she had a lover, but she had no growth and the past was her front and center.

It showed in the hurt she spewed out in stories and attitude the more we spoke.

Two hours, food, and one diet soda later, I smiled, and went home. I hugged her tight, said my goodbyes, and have never met up again.

Now this isn't it say I don't send my love from afar or cheer her successes on. It just means I can't have my personal growth and keep the bullshit from my past.

My bullshit? Was holding onto a past that I so clearly had outgrown. Not just actions or thoughts that wouldn't leave, but the people.

I was no longer the same. I had outgrown the people, places, and stories. I will always have a past, but it made ME better for my present and my future. I'm able to share my past to teach, to enlighten, to give advice. Not to let it swallow me whole.

Let it go. Drop the bullshit. Get real. Forward March.

This means you will in fact have to FORGIVE, have some self realization moments that aren't pretty, and maybe throw away those old pics.

4. Alone Is Not Lonely

I feel like this hard truth, is one we all know but sometimes don't put into motion.

I dated a man, who was constantly on his phone, playing video games, and being (for lack of better wording) a complete stoner-douche bag. When all I wanted was to go out of the house, to concerts, dancing, movie dates.

When we did go out, I had to often pay because though he could afford his pot, he never had money for dates. I am a firm believer in women can pay, but no man should be a kept man by refusing to better himself. Struggle while bettering yourself?

Okay. But this guy was just a lazy guy who spent most convos trying to make me feel less than to make himself feel better. Like he was a prize to be won.

Trust me they don't give prizes in hell, so clearly I hadn't won a damn thing, when a partner pulls this mess, take my advice and walk away immediately.

I had a partner, I was supposed to be learning and exploring with him, instead I felt lonely right beside him. I hated that feeling. That feeling no one cared enough to reach out, or ask my opinion, or know my interests. I felt like I was unloved and it was a domino effect right back to an old mindset.

Truth, I was unloved. I was with the wrong person. I was with someone who ruled my loneliness and it gave me a fear of being alone.

Fun fact, they aren't the same.

Loneliness is a fucking mind game and a horrible slope to speed down. It leads to bad choices, impulsive choices. Depression and the enemy sneak in and feed your dark thoughts. Thoughts of you are not good enough, worthy. Thoughts you deserve what you're getting.

Do. Not. Listen.

You are worthy. You are loved. You are great.

And you know when I found this out most? When I was ALONE.

I left the (in their own mind) hometown heroes, mind numbing, soul sucking people, I left the bad situations, and each time I was alone.

It wasn't until I came home after that coke-Nadia fueled weekend, single, and lost, I was finally able to recognize the power in being alone.

I was not lonely. I could read, I could watch whatever movie I wanted, I could find out my strengths, my dislikes.

I could eat ice cream for lunch. I could face myself.

And that I did. I spent a year, reading, working, shopping, dinners with my two Moms. I stayed out of bars and away from dating of any kind. I found power in being alone. I wasn't lonely, I was at peace. I was finally able to love the reflection the mirror shown back at me.

This is not to say I didn't have nights where tears fell, because I felt so far on the outside.

Or didn't have nights of why didn't anyone want to pick me?

Why am I doing this alone again????

I was growing, I was becoming the person, I needed and wanted to be. So to say it was just a simple few days of ice cream and chick flicks would be a lie.

In fact, it was a year before I really became completely self aware and completely mentally strong enough to no longer question being alone.

5. Faith.

In the days I chose to be alone, I had a friend invite me to his church.

I was extremely hesitant. God. Religion. Never in my cards. But I was turning over new leaf, I said ok, and off we went.

I was shocked, the band played a song by "The Who," the pastor had a biker beard, t shirt and jeans. Tattoos from his wrists up to his forearms.

He spoke of God like he was your friendly neighborhood Spider-Man. Like God was your very best friend, the one you invited to sleepovers and pizza and shared your secrets with. I felt, safe, warm, and enlightened, in a way I had never felt before. There was no judgement. No worries if you were a different color or sexual orientation. Just this open door, open arms, open heart, place with kind people singing, laughing and filled with faith.

I went home with almost a skip in my step. I didn't know what to really think or say. I told my friend, I actually enjoyed it.

"I'm here every Sunday," he replied.

Now, I will tell you the feeling deflated the next day...almost like not being fed enough. Or reaching for your delicious cup of coffee to find you have just a drop left.

I wanted that feeling back. It fed me so much more than a snack or random romance novel.

But me being me, hesitant with all things God and religion. I didn't know where to begin so I googled "relatable stories about finding God for women,"

I stumbled upon a book called "The Lipstick Gospel," by the ever wonderful Stephanie May Wilson.

This story made God feel closer, like the best friend feeling notion I had before. It was funny, relatable, and real. There was a quote that stuck with me;

"I always thought the Bible was more of a Salad thing, but it isn't. It's a chocolate thing." - Donald

Miller , BlueLike Jazz: Nonreligious Thoughts on Christian Spirituality

Just like that, I started reading more and finding my own faith. Forming my own relationship with God.

NOT religion.

I'm not here to bash religion. I'm here to tell you after making my way though a personal hell, religion and God aren't the same. Nor will they ever be.

I had that church I was fond of , but there wasn't denomination, there weren't rules or judgment. Nor do I make it every Sunday or am I criticized for it.

But every day my fuel is coffee and convo with God. Reading a devotional, or parts of the Bible I'm curious about. It isn't a race or this amazing feat, I just simply felt..better.

Layers of hurt and confusion melted away. I was more comfortable, in charge of myself, and learned to put worry and anxiety and trauma, with God and leave it there.

Faith is the hardest most rewarding feeling, action, I have ever encountered.

It didn't mean perfection and judgment. It didn't mean I was going to start preaching to you or choking you with alarming facts and views if I thought you weren't living right. I will tell you to pray, to have faith, to breathe, I'm not going to judge you, because I'm imperfect and learning.

Faith to me meant winning or losing the day, you still had the faith to believe and carry on.

God was still the best friend you're sharing pizza with, he just wasn't the best friend who was going to coddle and give you what you wanted. He gave you what you needed.

Weeks went by, months went by, two years of being alone, one year of being alone with a new found faith, I felt like I was completely reborn.

6. Love.

What I knew about love then....Love had been anything but easy...love had been painful, fun, sleazy, long, lustful, love had been wrong, right, and it left me bruised and broke.

Love wasn't any of things. I was. I was at one time, all of those things and much, much, more.

Love isn't the hurt you feel after the broken heart.

Love isn't to blame when your lover has scorned you.

Love is what carries you through to be better for the next person.

Love is what makes you stay strong for your children when your weak.

I had to fall in love with my flaws, my bad and my good to really heal.

Love for me looked differently nowadays.

I had lied, cheated, stole, broken hearts, been broken, bled, cried, and here I was. I had found God the same time I had found the devil and it had been a hell of a ride.

I knew love for me was not slow dances, but salsa music and jumping to punk rock in the kitchen.

I knew love for me now, was little smiles and summer nights. Days spent by a beach and listening to the waves crash. Love wasn't confusing, abusive, or a race.

Love was simple.

Black and white, no grey area. Love wasn't a lover who left you hanging. Or a lover who told you you're butt needed to look better or your toes needed to be red. Love wasn't a lover who only saw your worth if you were benefiting them.

Love was 100/100, not 50/50.

I had accepted all that I was (and wasn't) from loving myself to faith. I was at the most stable season of my life, I had ever been in, this is when love walked into my life.

This time love came in the form of a man and four amazing children.

I was able to love someone with commitment, with compromise, and respect. He wasn't telling me what I should be or leaving me in my own head. He was holding my hand and telling me corny jokes. He was dancing with me in the kitchen and coaching our kids in sports and being the father they loved.

He was accepting my views and strong enough to still have his own. He let me hold onto him as long as I wanted, he went to movies and ate late night snacks with me, we were able to raise these children with open hearts and minds.

I was able to share my stories with our kiddos and give them life lessons on the stories that could wait. I was cooking dinner, and eating ice cream (on a couch much to small),but we all snuggled in together anyways to watch Disney movies and our favorite shows.

The End.

All that chaos, those bad choices, the days that were to long, were worth it. There wasn't some miraculous bolt of lightening that zapped me back to reality after all the bad episodes. This was a literal mind fuck of a journey that I was lucky enough to come out on the other side of. There was no curtain up, applause, this was life.

In the days I spent alone, I used to dwell on the wrong I had done to others, causing a constant conflict inside myself. In the end , I had to forgive myself, and though I had reached out to some, to extend my apologies over the events I could remember , it will never be the same.

That's ok, sometimes forgiving yourself is all you can do.

Lessons learned and even though, I had sought forgiveness, issued the apologies, I had to accept the truth for what it was and move forward.

Plus, even in the truth setting you "free," you gotta know you can't control how others see you. I had come full circle, found myself, love, God, made good of my wrongs, and there are still people who still cross the street to avoid me.

Some because well , let's face it, we all made mistakes then (and seeing me was a reminder), others, don't believe in forgiveness, and most because I had simply cut them to deep.

In the end, all of my bad taught me to be a better human, partner, friend, mother, daughter. I would not change my life (past or present) for anything.

What I do know? 100%? If you take anything from this?

Live free.

Don't hurt people.

Be honest even if it hurts.

Live to make memories, not nights you'll regret. Travel often.

Fall in love with yourself before anyone else.

Grab onto some morals and keep them.

Have faith.

Do whatever the fuck makes you happy and in doing so don't step on anyone or anything to get there, take the good road less travel and enjoy that damn ride.

Made in the USA
Middletown, DE
25 August 2021